She Persisted
in Sports

American Olympians
Who Changed
the Game

"Never underestimate the power of dreams and the influence of the human spirit . . . The potential for greatness lives within each of us."

"A champion is someone who has fallen off the horse a dozen times and gotten back on the horse a dozen times. Successful people never give up."

"The French girls apparently misunderstood the nature of the game . . . and turned up to play in high heels and tight skirts!"

"In this journey, the fear creeps in from time to time . . . I don't choose to live there; I let it spark me . . ."

"I am a full woman and I'm strong; and I'm powerful, and I'm beautiful at the same time."

"It's important to me that youth everywhere, no matter their race, religion, or gender, know that anything is possible is possible if you choose to do . . . it's okay to have a dream and aspire to do something and go for it."

"That medal . . . really symbolizes a lot more than just two weeks of hockey."

"You can't win them all but you can try."

"All my life I've dreamed in gold."

"Records are always meant to be broken."

"Whatever it is you choose to do . . ."

"Think it, be it."

"You can't win them all but you can try."

"A champion is someone who has fallen off the horse a dozen times"

"People said women couldn't swim the Channel, but I proved they could."

"with perseverance."

"You have to believe in yourself when no one else does. That makes you a winner right there."

"To go out there and prove what I can do has taught me a lot about who I am."

"There is no substitute for hard work."

Written by
Chelsea Clinton

Illustrated by
Alexandra Boiger

PHILOMEL BOOKS

Philomel Books
An imprint of Penguin Random House LLC, New York

First published in the United States of America by Philomel,
an imprint of Penguin Random House LLC, 2020.
Text copyright © 2020 by Chelsea Clinton.
Illustrations copyright © 2020 by Alexandra Boiger.

Philomel Books is a registered trademark of Penguin Random House LLC.

Visit us online at penguinrandomhouse.com

Library of Congress Cataloging-in-Publication Data is available upon request.

Printed in the United States of America.
ISBN 9780593114544
10 9 8 7 6 5 4 3 2 1

Edited by Jill Santopolo.
Design by Ellice M. Lee.
Text set in ITC Kennerley.
The art was done in watercolor and ink on Fabriano paper, then edited in Photoshop.

For Charlotte, Aidan, Jasper & kids
everywhere with Olympic and
non-Olympic dreams —C.C.

To Andrea, with love —A.B.

It's not easy to be a girl athlete. Girls are more likely to be told sports are for boys. Or that they'll never be good enough, fast enough, strong enough and that their athletic dreams are unacceptable, even impossible. Don't listen to those people.

These woman athletes made their sports dreams real.

They persisted.

When MARGARET IVES ABBOTT was
young, in the late 1800s, some girls had to work, and some girls,
including Margaret, went to school. It was rare for any girl to
play sports, but Margaret played golf. Even though she won
local tournaments, there weren't many opportunities for girls to
compete on a bigger stage. Still, **she persisted** in practicing
golf while she studied and traveled. When she was in Paris in
1900, Margaret and her mother learned of an international sports
exhibition happening at the World's Fair. Without knowing that
it was the second modern Olympic Games, they entered and
Margaret won! When Margaret died in 1955, she had no idea she'd
been the first American woman to become an Olympic champion.

"The French girls apparently misunderstood the nature of the game . . . and turned up to play in high heels and tight skirts!"

When she was a child, GERTRUDE EDERLE lost part of her hearing because of measles, but she and her parents were determined that it wouldn't stop her from doing anything she wanted, including swimming. By the time she turned twenty, she had won three medals in freestyle at the 1924 Olympics. She then found a new dream: to swim the English Channel. After Gertrude's first attempt didn't succeed, her coach said that women might just not be capable of swimming the Channel. Rather than listen to that coach, she found a new coach, and **she persisted**. The next year, in 1926, she succeeded; her record time would not be broken for more than twenty years.

"People said women couldn't swim the Channel, but I proved they could."

When she was a teenager, MILDRED "BABE" DIDRIKSON ZAHARIAS worked as a seamstress, sewing sacks to store things like grains, potatoes or sand, and at an insurance company. Babe could have decided she had no time for sports, but she persisted in playing alongside her brothers; she earned her nickname, which honored the famous baseball player Babe Ruth, after hitting five home runs in one game. Her training clearly paid off: at the 1932 Olympics, Babe won gold medals in javelin and the 80-meter hurdles and a silver medal in the high jump. After her Olympic triumph, Babe took up golf and went on to win ten major women's golf championships; she is considered one of the greatest woman athletes ever.

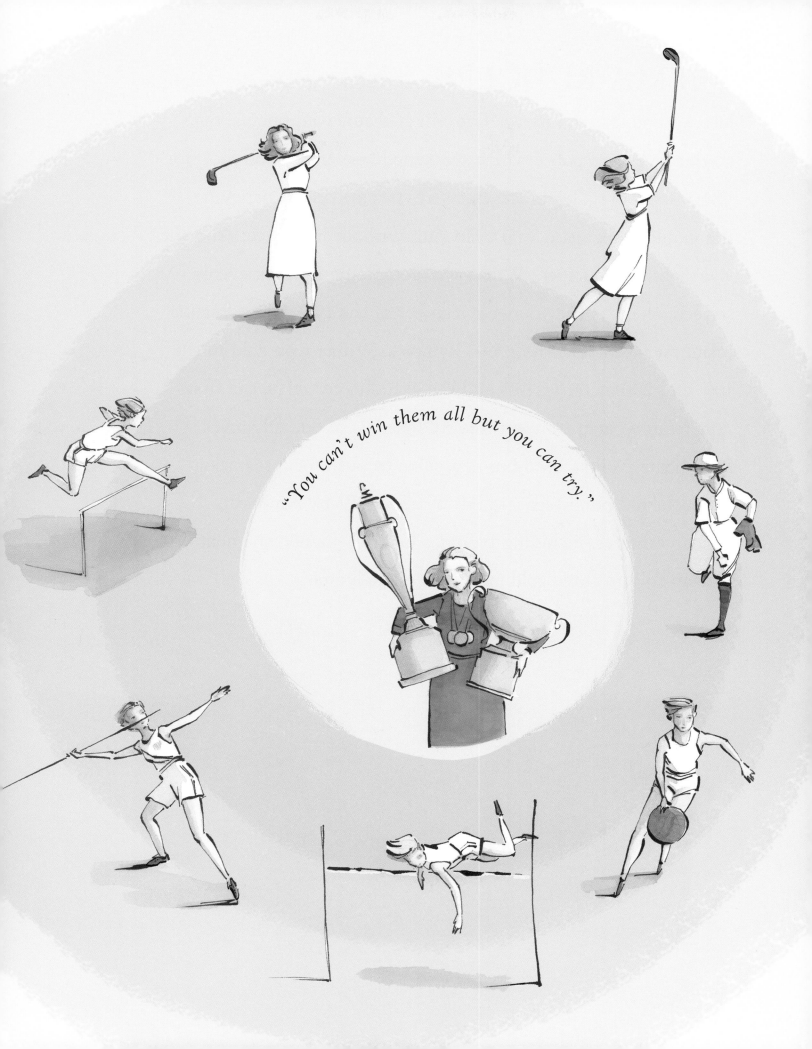

"You can't win them all but you can try."

WILMA RUDOLPH was born prematurely, weighing just 4.5 pounds, and by age five, she had survived pneumonia, scarlet fever and polio, which weakened her left leg and foot; for years, she wore a leg brace. But she persisted in believing she would walk again, and even run, without her brace. And she was right! By fourteen, Wilma was competing in track events. At sixteen, she was the youngest member of the 1956 U.S. Olympic team. At twenty, at the 1960 Olympics, Wilma won gold in the 100- and 200-meter sprints and the 4x100-meter relay, the first American woman to win three gold medals in one Olympics. Back home, Wilma used her new fame to push for integration in sports and public spaces and to support Black American woman athletes, including Florence Griffith Joyner, the next woman to win three gold medals in one Olympics.

"Never underestimate the power of dreams
and the influence of the human spirit . . .
The potential for greatness lives within each of us."

Born with spina bifida, a condition in which the spine is not fully formed, JEAN DRISCOLL started playing wheelchair sports in high school. While playing wheelchair basketball at the University of Illinois, Jean realized her real passion and talents were in wheelchair racing. She participated in four Paralympic Games, starting at the 1988 Summer Olympics, winning twelve medals, including five golds. Jean also won eight Boston Marathons, more than any other athlete ever. She could have rested on her personal and team achievements, yet **she persisted** in bringing her love of sports to other athletes with disabilities around the world, including helping to start Ghana's first Paralympic team.

"A champion is someone who has fallen off the horse a dozen times and gotten back on the horse a dozen times. Successful people never give up."

When MIA HAMM and other women on the 1996 Olympic soccer team started playing their sport, there were few role models for them to look up to. Soccer wasn't a particularly popular sport in the U.S., and most of the attention was given to men. MIA HAMM, CARLA OVERBECK, JULIE FOUDY, KRISTINE LILLY, BRANDI CHASTAIN, BRIANA SCURRY and the other members of their team could have given up at any point, but **they persisted**, traveling the country and the world proving that American women could win. They earned a gold medal at the first Olympics to include women's soccer and, a few years later, won the World Cup! Mia and her teammates proved American girls could play soccer and win. Girls' soccer is now one of the most popular kids' sports in America.

"There is no substitute for hard work." —Mia Hamm

Born with clubfoot, KRISTI YAMAGUCHI had to wear casts to help turn her feet so they would point forward. When she was six years old, Kristi saw her older sister figure skating and she wanted to be on the ice, too; her parents first supported her lessons as a form of physical therapy for her still-recovering feet. Although her sister stopped skating, **she persisted** in training harder and harder on the ice. As a teenager, she won medals in both singles and pairs skating. With the 1992 Olympics looming, she decided to focus on her singles skating. It was a good decision. She won both the Olympic gold and the World Championships that year.

"Whatever it is you choose to do . . . it's okay to have a dream and aspire to do something and go for it."

Together, tennis-star sisters VENUS and SERENA WILLIAMS have won fourteen women's doubles titles across all four Grand Slam tournaments, and three Olympic gold medals, starting at the 2000 Summer Olympics. They are one of the most successful doubles teams of all time. In their individual careers, Venus has won seven Grand Slams and Serena twenty-three; they have also both won individual golds at two different Olympics. The Williams sisters have confronted vile racism and sexism throughout their careers, but that never stopped them. **They persisted** in pursuing a sport they love and have helped define what tennis is for young girls, and boys, everywhere.

"You have to believe in yourself when no one else does. That makes you a winner right there."
—Venus Williams

"I am a full woman and I'm strong, and I'm powerful, and I'm beautiful at the same time."
—Serena Williams

Both MISTY MAY-TREANOR and KERRI WALSH JENNINGS had played, and won, multiple team volleyball events by the time they each graduated from college. They both then shifted their focus to women's beach volleyball, began working together and dominated the sport. At both the 2004 and 2008 Olympics, they won gold medals, but after Kerri gave birth to two children in less than a year, many people wondered if the two of them would play together again. They persisted in playing as a team, though, and at the 2012 Olympics, while Kerri was pregnant with her third child, she and Misty won again, showing the world that mothers can win gold medals, too.

"All my life I've dreamed in gold."

—Misty May-Treanor

"In this journey, the fear creeps in
from time to time. . . . I don't choose
to live there; I let it spark me."

—Kerri Walsh Jennings

When DIANA TAURASI began playing basketball as a girl in the 1980s, professional women's basketball didn't exist in the United States and women's basketball was a relatively new Olympic sport (even though men had been playing since 1936). Rather than be discouraged by the lack of opportunities, **she persisted** in working hard on the court. In college, she led her team to three championships in a row. Diana went on to win four Olympic gold medals with the American Women's Basketball Team, starting at the 2004 Summer Olympics, and three WNBA championships with the Phoenix Mercury. She is the WNBA's all-time leading scorer.

"Records are always meant to be broken."

When
SIMONE BILES

was six years old, she and her sister
were adopted by their grandparents. On a field
trip to a local gymnastics center that year, Simone
began imitating the gymnasts. The coach noticed and asked
for permission for Simone to join their program. She did—and
she persisted, throwing herself into every aspect of her new
sport. She was the first American gymnast to win a medal in every
event and now has many difficult gymnastic skills named after her.
At the 2016 Summer Olympics, Simone won four gold medals
and one bronze, and has won more than twenty Olympic and
World Championship medals in her career. She is widely
recognized as the greatest gymnast of all time.

"To go out there and prove what I can do has taught me a lot about who I am."

While she was growing up, IBTIHAJ MUHAMMAD's parents wanted their daughter to be able to compete and excel in a sport that allowed her to remain fully covered and wear hijab to cover her head. At thirteen, Ibtihaj started to fence. Some people doubted that she could succeed, wondering if someone who wore hijab could ever be a champion. She persisted and proved the naysayers wrong. In college, she was an All-American athlete and later earned a spot on the United States National Fencing Team. At the 2016 Summer Olympics, Ibtihaj became the first hijab-wearing Muslim American to win an Olympic medal. She continued to shatter stereotypes when she helped design the first-ever hijab-wearing Barbie modeled on her!

"It's important to me
that youth everywhere,
no matter their
race, religion, or
gender, know that
anything is possible
with perseverance."

Growing up in North Dakota, all six Lamoureux siblings played hockey, including the youngest, identical twins JOCELYNE and MONIQUE LAMOUREUX. When they were twelve, the sisters joined the local boys' team and, as the only girls, **they persisted** in leading their team to the state championship. They both were women's hockey stars in high school and college and made the 2010 and 2014 U.S. Olympic Women's Hockey teams, taking home the silver at both games. But things were different at the 2018 PyeongChang Winter Olympics. In the final game, Monique scored the necessary goal to send the match into overtime. Then the match went to a shootout. Jocelyne scored the game-winning goal, and the sisters helped the U.S. Women's Hockey team take home their first gold in twenty years.

"That medal . . . really
symbolizes a lot more than
just two weeks of hockey."
—Jocelyne Lamoureux

"Think it, be it."
—Monique Lamoureux

So if someone tells you girls can't be athletes
or that you'll never make it, don't listen.
Focus on your dreams.
These women did just that.

They persisted and so should you.